Heather & Avery

and the

Bicycle Shop

Written by

Illustrator

Scriptor House LLC

2810 N Church St Wilmington, Delaware, 19802

www.scriptorhouse.com

Phone: +1302-205-2043

Published by Scriptor House LLC

Paperback ISBN: 979-8-88692-052-9

eBook ISBN: 979-8-88692-053-6

Heather and Avery are cousins.

Heather likes little ponies, swings,
and playing with Avery.

Avery likes basketball, slides, and
playing with Heather.

Heather and Avery are best friends.

One sunny morning Heather and Avery
rode their bicycles up and down
the sidewalk.

Avery kept riding faster and faster,
twisting and turning his bike and
trying to do the fancy moves of
the bigger boys.

"Watch out, Avery," said Heather.

"You are going to fall off your bike."

Avery didn't stop until

. . .*C R A S H*. . . .

Avery fell one way, while the bike went the
other and slammed into a tree.

"Owww!" cried Avery. "I could have done
it if that crack wasn't in the sidewalk."

"Are you okay? Oh, Avery, look at your bike!" said Heather, as she and Avery ran to the tree.

The bike frame was scratched, the chain hung off the sprocket, and the bent, flat front wheel had fallen off the bike.

Heather and Avery grabbed for the wheel at the same time. All of a sudden, in a WHOOSH and a WHIRL. . .

Heather and Avery were standing in front of a small shop with wheels and gears in the window.

They saw a man riding up the street on something strange. He used the pedals like a bike, but the front wheel was huge, while the back wheel was tiny.

The man stopped, climbed off his big bike, and said, "Oh my! That wheel needs to be straightened. Why don't you come into the shop here and my brother and I will try to fix it?"

As Heather and Avery entered the shop, they saw several strange looking bikes. Some of the bikes were put together and others were in a lot of pieces.

In the corner, they noticed a bike with things that looked like wings.

Avery asked "What is this place and where are we?"

"You are in The Wright Cycle Company in Dayton, Ohio. My brother Orville and I fix, make, and sell bicycles here. My name is Wilber Wright. What are your names?"

"I am Heather and he is Avery. Why is that bike wheel so big?"

"The simplest answer is to go farther faster," replied Wilber. "Orville, do you want to show them how?"

"Of course I do, Wilber. Children, step over here."

Heather and Avery walked to the back of the shop. Orville gave Heather a baseball and Avery a marble.

"As you children can see, both are round, but the baseball is much bigger than the marble" he began. "Now place them on this board." They did.

Orville raised one end of the board until the baseball and marble began to move.

"Since the baseball is larger than the marble, it covers more space," said Orville. "Once they start to roll, the baseball rolls over more of the board quicker than the marble, so it reaches the end faster."

"The wheel on the bicycle does the same. It covers more road faster than a smaller wheel," added Wilber.

"But, it is so high. Aren't you afraid you will fall off?" Avery asked.

Both Orville and Wilber laughed.

"Avery, we do fall off a lot," Wilber replied.

"In fact, when we ride downhill we go so fast that we put our legs over the handlebars for a smoother ride, or to jump off if we need to!"

"You must break a lot of wheels," Avery said.

"We do have a busy bicycle shop," Orville answered, as the brothers laughed harder.

Pointing to the bike in the corner, Heather asked, "Why does that bike have wings?"

"Have you ever watched birds fly?" Wilber began. "When they want to turn in the air they lean into the turn, just like a person riding a bicycle."

"Birds also change the angle of their wings so they can tip one way or the other, working with the wind. We are trying to make a flying machine that can do the same thing."

"The flyer will have control so the wind will not make him crash," Orville added.

"But only one person can fly on a bike with wings,"
said Avery. "Why don't you just buy a ticket to
ride on a big airplane?"

Orville and Wilber looked at each other
and said
"Buy a ticket. . . ?"

All of a sudden, in a WHIRL and a WHOOSH, Heather and Avery were on the sidewalk with Avery's bike fixed.

"Let's fly down the street!" shouted Avery. They pedaled off, not knowing that they had just witnessed a piece of history.

Ravey the Hare's

The Wright Brothers

1817	The "Walking Machine" was invented–2 wheels with cross-board, no pedals or handlebars— by Baron von Drais of Germany.
1865	The "boneshaker", or Velocipede, has pedals mounted to the front wheel for the rider to propel the machine with the feet off the ground.
1867	Wilbur is born on April 16, near Millville, Indiana.
1871	Orville is born on August 19, in Dayton, Ohio.
1873	The first high-wheel bicycle has rubber tires mounted on metal rims.
1886	Orville starts a printing business.
1889	Orville publishes a newspaper called the *West Side News* and Wilbur joins him as its editor.
1892	Wright Cycle Company is formed.
1896	Wilbur and Orville take an interest in the "flying problem."
1900	The Wrights travel to Kitty Hawk to test their first glider.
1901	The Wrights build a wind tunnel and test different wing shapes.
1903	On December 17th Orville makes the first controlled, sustained powered flight
1904-1905	Wilbur and Orville develop the first practical airplane just outside of Dayton.
1911	The Wright's airplane *Vin Fiz* crosses the United States in 84 days.
1912	Wilbur Wright dies of typhoid fever. He is 45 years of age.
1918	Orville Wright pilots a plane for the last time for a celebration in Dayton, Ohio.
1920	President Woodrow Wilson appoints Orville to the National Advisory Committee for Aeronautics (NACA, the forerunner of NASA).
1942	Orville Wright and the National Cash Register Co assist the U.S. Navy to create a code-breaking machine that will decipher encrypted German communications.
1944	Orville Wright has his last airplane ride, piloted by Howard Hughes.
1948	Orville Wright dies of a heart attack at the age of 77.

www.ingramcontent.com/pod-product-compliance
Lightning Source LLC
Chambersburg PA
CBHW081922120726
47996CB00010B/3435